Nutcracker

Dancing Shapes

Shapes and Stories

from Konora's

Twenty-Five

Nutcracker

Roles

Nutcracker Dancing Shapes: Shapes and Stories from Konora's Twenty-Five Nutcracker Roles

Summary: Join Konora as she looks back through her twenty-five Nutcracker roles and explore the shapes she creates with her body. Konora leads readers through the story of *The Nutcracker*, her personal *Nutcracker* experiences, storytelling and imagination, ballet shapes, and some funny things that happened along the way.

ISBN: 978-1-7363536-3-9

JUVENILE NONFICTION: Performing Arts: Dance (PERFORMING ARTS: Dance: Classical & Ballet)

First Edition

Other *Once Upon a Dance* titles:

Dancing Shapes

More Dancing Shapes

Dancing Shapes with Attitude

Konora's Shapes

More Konora's Shapes

Ballerina Dreams Ballet Inspiration Journal/Notebook

Dancing Shapes Ballet Inspiration Journal/Notebook

Joey Finds His Jump!

Petunia Perks Up

This book is dedicated to

Wade Heninger and

Emerald Ballet Theatre teachers, staff, and volunteers.

Hello Fellow Dancer,

As usual, I have a lot to tell you, and I've crammed in a bunch of mini-chapters.

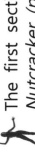 The first section is about me and my personal experiences with *The Nutcracker*. *(page 6)*

 We'll go through the basic story of *The Nutcracker* and the distinct plots I've seen at various company productions. *(page 9)*

 I'll tell you about my all-time favorite roles. *(page 16)*

 Please remember to warm up your muscles and body before dancing. *(page 22)*

Let's act out the story next. I'll talk you through the highlights and some of the best places to bring out your inner storyteller. *(page 23)*

We'll talk ballet terms and learn just a little *fancy French*. *(page 27)*

 Next up, we'll look at more *Nutcracker* shapes from a few more performance pictures. *(page 31)*

 We'll wrap up with a few stories that remind us mistakes happen and not to take ourselves too seriously. *(page 35)*

 If you want to learn more about the French ballet terms, there's a section at the end with translations and how I would pronounce the words. *(page 41)*

 I've left a few extra shapes and jumps on the opposite page for another time. I like to include a few duplicates from the story's pages so you can think about the details and whether you've seen them before. You might also recognize a couple poses from our other books.

So, are you ready to talk dance? Let's go!

Part One

Twenty-Five Roles!

Photo: Wade Heninger/Heninger Fotographik.
Thank you, Emerald Ballet Theatre.

Once Upon a Dance, a little girl was lucky enough to be cast in the dream role of Clara in *The Nutcracker*. It was a huge surprise, and she was very honored. Who knows, maybe this was where her ballerina dreams started to take hold.

My mom and I tried to list all the *Nutcracker* roles I've learned over the years. We counted twenty-five different parts! She told me a few I'd forgotten about, and she thought she might be missing one or two. That got me reminiscing about all those different *Nutcrackers*, silly things that happened, and the choreography and people involved. With five different studios' productions of this holiday classic, it's honestly a little hard keeping them all straight.

I've danced in *Nutcrackers* for literally as long as I can remember. This year, 2020, will be different because most ballet companies and schools have decided not to do an in-person performance. At Ballet Idaho, where I've danced the last couple months, we're learning a holiday show that will be sent out for people to watch at home. Even though it's weird to not be doing *Nutcracker*, it's super fun choreography, and it might be nice to have a little time off.

My family never had time to do many of the Christmas traditions other families enjoy. In fact, the last few years, they've visited me between shows just to spend some holiday time with me in Colorado, New Mexico, Utah, Washington, and Idaho.

Spending many months living, thinking, and breathing *Nutcracker* is definitely my typical Christmas. It seems perfectly normal, but when I think about it, I guess it's a pretty crazy life. Ballet companies often start working on *Nutcracker* choreography as soon as they're back in the studio after summer vacation. For lead roles, I'd start working in the summer before school even started.

Many companies have *Nutcracker* performances from Thanksgiving all the way through New Year's. One year at Pacific Northwest Ballet (PNB), the company did forty-two performances! The dancers take turns so no one gets too tired. With so many performances, a few people might need a break because of injuries, so it's important to have understudies, people who learn the role just in case. I think there were at least sixty of us who learned the Waltz of the Flowers at PNB!

Photo: ©Angela Sterling. Thank you, Pacific Northwest Ballet.

Part Two

What an
Odd Story!

Photo: Wade Heninger/Heninger Fotographik.
Thank you, Emerald Ballet Theatre.

It's really quite odd that there are so many productions about this very strange-looking doll. A long time ago, people used these dolls to crack nuts, but I don't think anyone's used nutcrackers for cracking nuts in decades.

I thought it would be fun to show you some decorative nutcrackers. Which do you like best?

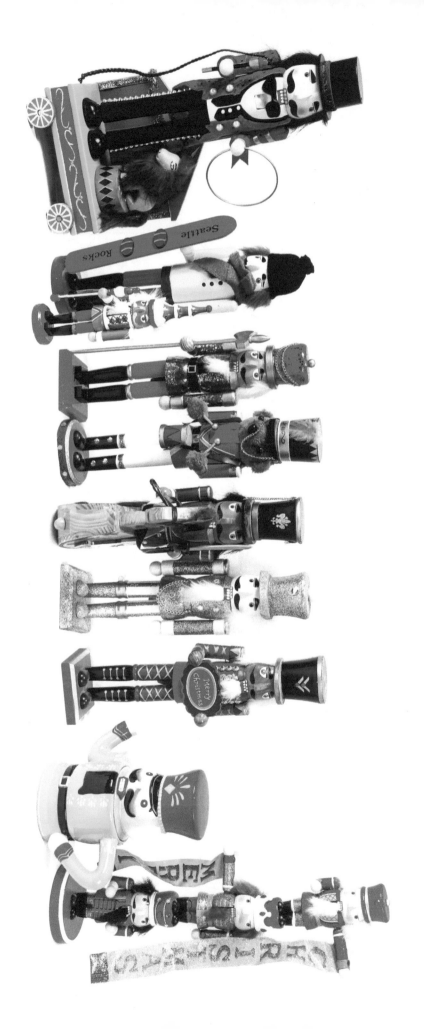

I've danced in a pile of *Nutcrackers*, and they were all different, but most of the stories go something like this:

- A girl named Clara, her brother Fritz, and her family host a party.

- At the party, there are typical festivities and some amazing life-size dancing dolls that entertain everyone. There are also presents, and Clara gets a nutcracker from a mystery guest, Herr Drosselmeyer.

- In most versions, Fritz breaks the nutcracker, but it gets fixed up as good as new.

- Later that night, the Nutcracker comes to life, calls in his army, and battles a group of huge mice who have come into the house with a king or queen as their leader.

- There's usually something weird that occurs with the stage props to demonstrate there's crazy magic happening. Often, the Christmas tree or the entire room becomes gigantic.

- Clara helps by distracting the mouse leader, and the Nutcracker kills it. (It makes me a little sad each time the mouse leader dies.)

- The Nutcracker often turns into a prince. He and Clara travel together through a swirling scene of beautiful snowflakes to a special land where they meet festive characters who perform dances.

Photos this page: Wade Heninger/Heninger Fotographik. Thank you, Roman Zinovyev and Emerald Ballet Theatre.

At Emerald Ballet Theatre (EBT), where I grew up dancing, Clara helps the Nutcracker Prince defeat the Mouse Queen by hitting her with a candle. Little Clara becomes a grown-up version of herself when she visits the special Land of Sweets. At the end of the story, we see that the uncle who gave her the doll was responsible for the adventure, and he turns her back into her younger self again after it's over.

At PNB, it's a similar story, except Clara stays little the whole time. Everything gets gigantic, including the Nutcracker's bed, which they later ride around in the snow. Clara helps distract the Mouse King by throwing her shoe. Her Nutcracker Prince turns out to be a boy she met at her family's party, and they ride away at the end in an awesome sled with reindeer.

Ballet Idaho's version starts similarly with a party. The dolls come to life, and the story elements from the party carry into Clara's dream visit to the Land of Sweets.

Photo: ©Angela Sterling. Thank you, Pacific Northwest Ballet.

Photo above: Wade Heninger/Heninger Fotographik.

Opposite: Sharen Bradford, The Dancing Image. Thank you, Aspen Santa Fe Ballet.

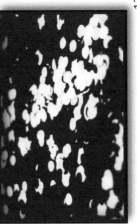

The snow scene is probably the most consistent across shows. It almost always involves snowflakes in beautiful dresses dancing in intricate patterns with lots of jumps, runs, and poses. There's usually some type of stage snow falling. It got stuck up my nose and in my eyelashes. I've even eaten a snowflake or two; it was gross. But it's so magical! Here's a picture of actual snow they used at PNB.

The second act of the story is where things go in all different directions. Each version has its own take on the characters, often related to food like hot chocolate, tea, and coffee, but not always.

In the Ballet West production, instead of tea, there was a Chinese dragon. I had a very small part; I was two legs of the dragon. It was tricky to keep all together with six of us under a dragon. We had to wear gardening gloves because it was hard to hold the huge puppet steady. But it was very cool for the audience to see, and they enjoyed it.

Aspen Santa Fe's version is like a circus, and there's a huge merry-go-round. The dances are very different, and there are many props that dancers carry or use. There are dancers dancing with ribbons, a trapeze silk artist who hangs from the ceiling, and a flamenco dancer, a traditional dancer from Spain.

So, there you go, five distinct stories from five companies. There must be a gazillion interpretations. It's crazy that the story has become such a mainstay of the ballet world, with millions of people coming back for their traditional holiday ballet celebration each year.

Photo: Sharen Bradford, The Dancing Image. Thank you, Aspen Santa Fe Ballet.

Part Three

My Favorites

When I was growing up, another dancer's dad took pictures of all our shows. I think he might be my mom's favorite person. My show pictures are on the walls of her house. It's strange walking by my dancing history each time I go to bed while visiting, but they seem to make her happy. My EBT teachers, along with the photographer's pictures of me as a baby snowflake to Little Clara to Sugar Plum, are the reason we could make this book.

All photos this spread: Wade Heninger/Heninger Fotographik.
Thank you, Emerald Ballet Theatre (EBT), Artistic Director Viktoria Titova.

I've had so many amazing parts over the years in all these varied productions, but if I had to pick a favorite role, it might be Arabian. It's a long duet, a dance for two people, and your partner always lifts you up in beautiful shapes that are really fun. The Arabian dancer is sort of serious and mysterious, which was an interesting character to play.

All photos this spread: Wade Heninger/Heninger Fotographik. Thank you, Roman Zinovyev and Emerald Ballet Theatre.

At the very end of this Arabian version, my partner, who was my teacher at EBT, would spin me as I did a *pirouette* (turning while holding your leg in a *passé* position).

One time I counted, and I went around sixteen times! He was an amazing partner!

My last year at EBT, I was the Sugar Plum Fairy. They hired someone from outside the studio to perform Sugar Plum's partner. When it was time to rehearse the day before the show, the only time I got to practice with my new partner, I was sick with a cold. It wasn't my best performance, but there's an expression for theater: "The show must go on."

Photos this page: Wade Heninger/Heninger Fotographik.
Thank you, Nukri Mamistvalov and Emerald Ballet Theatre.

When I danced in PNB's *Nutcracker*, many families and teachers from Emerald Ballet came to see the shows. I had one teacher who always thought to take pictures, and she organized all these people for a picture after a performance. It's a special memory.

It was an honor to be Sugar Plum. These are pictures from after one of the shows. I had many friends and family come see me. It was so nice of everyone to be so supportive. Some of them even brought me flowers.

Thank you, the Pink Tights Gang, for all the pictures and all the love. Thank you, Sarah.

Warming Up

It's a good idea to warm up your body and muscles before you dance. Here are some ideas:

1) If you know some ballet basics, do *pliés* and *relevés* in *first, second,* and *third positions*. Then for each leg, do five *tendus* each direction and five *passés*. If you don't know these words, simply bend and straighten your knees ten times then run or march in place, lifting your knees extra high.

2) Give all of your parts a gentle jiggle or shake:
- your hands
- your arms
- your feet
- your legs
- your head
- your shoulders
- your back

3) Reach up high, then bend over and try to touch the floor.

4) Draw ten circles in the air using your shoulders as your paintbrushes.

5) Draw circles using each elbow as a paintbrush. Make five little ones and five big ones with each elbow.

6) Draw five little and five gigantic circles with each hand as your paintbrush.

(We practiced the listed dance moves in the first two Dancing Shapes books.)

Part Four

Act
It
Out

If you happened to read *More Dancing Shapes*, we talked about how storytelling helps dancers feel more connected to their characters. Will you help me tell *The Nutcracker* using your body and acting skills? Let's start by imagining you're happy to greet your friends at the party. How do you look excited and welcoming?

Oh, there's dancing at this party. Put on your favorite music and enjoy. Oh boy, there's cake. Yum! You love cake!

Life-size dolls arrive and perform for the guests. How would you feel seeing each one? Would you be surprised? A little scared? Can you show how your face and body might look when you first see the dolls, and as you watch their amazing dances:

• There's a fighting doll holding swords.
• There's a ballerina doll that twirls around on her tiptoes and blows kisses.
• There's a doll that really likes to jump.
• There's a set of Harlequin dolls, which are sort of like Italian jesters.

Next, could you get up and perform a short doll dance? How do you think each doll would move? Many times, the dolls have to keep their faces without expression. It's hard to dance with your body while not expressing emotion with your face.

Photos this spread: Wade Heninger/Heninger Fotographik.
Thank you, Taylor, Roman Zinovyev, and Emerald Ballet Theatre.

You get a nutcracker for a present. You think it's the neatest doll ever. What a unique gift!

Your rotten brother or sister breaks your doll. How does that feel in your body? Don't worry too much, it turns out alright. Herr Drosselmeyer fixes the doll for you.

The party's over and you go to sleep. Can you curl up in your bed and relax after a busy, wild night?

What's that noise? I think it might be a huge mouse! Oh, you're scared! How do you move and how does your face look? Since the mouse part is so fun, pretend to be a silly mouse scampering around, causing mischief.

The soldiers march in. In all the versions I've seen, the soldiers are like dolls that don't have any expression; they move like robots.

There's the big fight. Do you want to be the Nutcracker or the Mouse Queen or King?

Photos this spread: Wade Heninger/Heninger Fotographik. Thank you, Taylor, Nukri Mamistvalov, and Emerald Ballet Theatre.

Imagine you are a fairy welcoming Clara. You are delicate and light on your feet because you have wings, and there's a magical feel to you.

There! If you acted out the story, you are officially a storyteller. I understand if you just want to enjoy the book the first time. You can always come back another time to re-create the story. You could even use a mirror or videotape yourself for fun.

Next, let's learn some ballet positions we often see in *The Nutcracker.*

Now the fight is over, and you are standing in a field of snow swirling all around you. It makes you want to dance your light-as-a-snowflake dance and jump and flit and spin around the room. (Be safe and careful.)

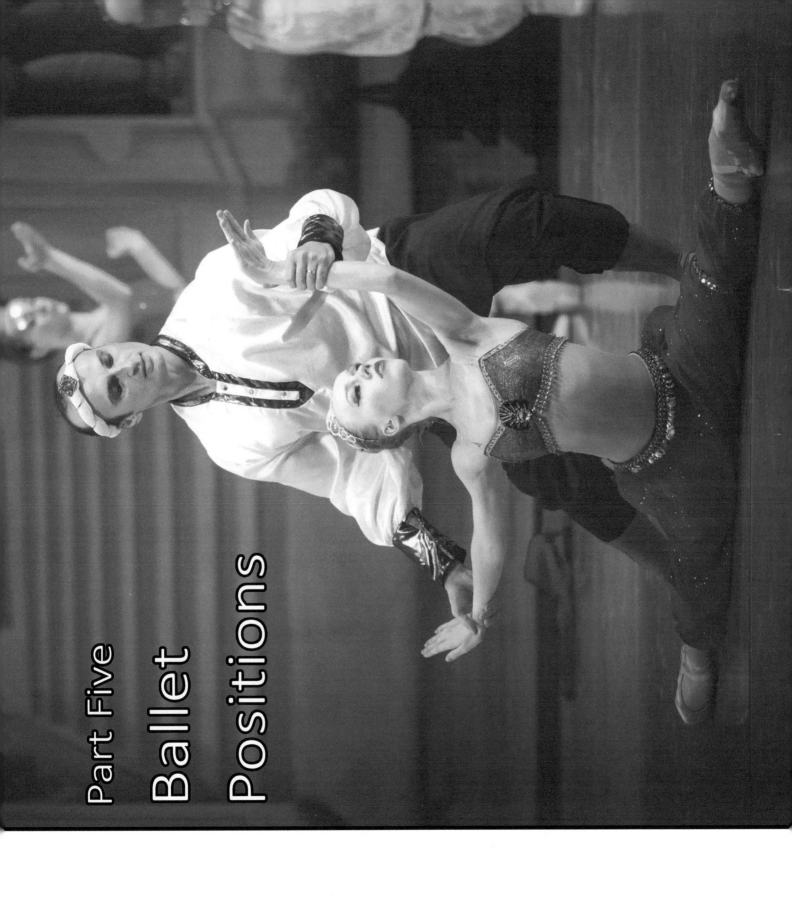

Part Five
Ballet
Positions

There are many ballet positions that I've seen over and over in *Nutcrackers* over the years. Let's look at three of them today.

Sous sus is like you are walking on a rope in the air while doing ballet. To make this shape, start with *first position* feet with your heels together and your toes facing out. Slide one foot in front of the other until your heel touches the big toe of your other foot. Next, lift your heels up while keeping most of the weight between your big toe and second toe. Then creep the front foot over so it's in front of the other. You're ready to walk the tightrope. The guests, the dolls, the Mouse Queen, Arabian, Sugar Plum, etc., all include *sous sus*.

Sous sus with arms in high fifth

We talked about weight and related feet positions and arms in Dancing Shapes.

Here come the soldiers and the Nutcracker himself. They're marching in using their parallel *passés*. The Mouse Queen and party guests also use this position. Lift your knee straight up as far as you can while keeping your hips still, your foot pointed, and your big toe touching the other leg. Be sure both knees point forward.

Parallel passé

Performance photos this spread: Wade Heninger/Heninger Fotographik. Thank you, Taylor, Roman Zinovyev, and Emerald Ballet Theatre.

I think the most popular step among *Nutcracker* shows might be the *arabesque*. Party children often do this pose. You've already seen my snow, Mouse Queen, and Arabian *arabesques*, and below is one from Sugar Plum. Snowflakes and flowers use *sauté arabesques*, jumps in the *arabesque* position, throughout both dances.

It's tricky to keep both legs straight and turned out while keeping your head and chest as upright as possible. In one of our other books, we suggest practicing *arabesque* by kneeling on the floor. With knees and hands touching the floor, lift your kitty tail up behind you with a straight, turned out leg and a pointed foot.

Arabesque

Performance photos this spread: Wade Heninger/Heninger Fotographik. Thank you, Nukri Mamistvalov and Emerald Ballet Theatre.

Do you want to try a few more *Nutcracker* shapes?

The hardest thing about being Little Clara was probably holding my arms in the beginning. I had to be a statue on stage for the first part of the show and stay there greeting guests as they arrived. How high can you count while holding this position?

For Little Clara, there were many *tendus* and *arabesques*. Above are tendus *devant* (to front) and *derrière* (to back).

Herr Drosselmeyer, the one who gives Clara the nutcracker, lifted me up for many *sauté arabesques*. I felt like I was flying! Later I had to do the same jump without help, which was harder.

One more Little Clara pose for you to try: the arms reaching up in a V, palms facing down and out.

Performance photos this spread: Wade Heninger/Heninger Fotographik. Thank you, Emerald Ballet Theatre.

Here are those same arms for a Mouse Queen *saut de chat.* To practice this *splits* shape, start on the floor. You could bend your front leg to make it a little easier. For Mouse Queen, I also made wide V-shaped legs on the Nutcracker's back. It was pretty fun doing a cartwheel on somebody and getting to dance with a sword. Also try this shape on the floor. Again, we are looking for straight, turned out legs with pointed feet.

Here's a picture of me as the Mouse Queen with my army of mice. Check out the V arms.

I had to hold this shape (notice the half V) for a really long time in PNB's snow. Do you remember the *fancy French* way to say behind?

EBT's Little Clara had this finale pose at the end of the show, holding the nutcracker in the spotlight. It was scary getting into that pose because I had to find my spot in the dark.

This pose might take some practice. If you haven't read my other books, I'm a big believer in the value of practice.

Clara photos: Wade Heninger/Heninger Fotographik. Thank you, Emerald Ballet Theatre.

Part Five
Stories and Mishaps

It's story time. I want to let you in on a few secrets because I think it's interesting to hear it's not all just glamour and beautiful dresses. There's so much hard work, and things don't always go as planned.

Thinking about that dramatic end pose reminded me that another Clara got hit in the head in the dark and was bleeding. I seem to have a few memories of head wounds and dancers trying not to get blood on that pretty white nightgown over the years.

I was thinking about other funny or scary *Nutcracker* happenings. Here are a few more:

• Since Clara is on stage for the whole first act, there are more chances something will go wrong. Another Clara mishap occurred when the candle broke on stage. We all had to finish the scene dancing around broken glass.

• My favorite story might be when Fritz threw up in the party scene. My friend was cast as a maid. She had to go onstage in character and clean it up while the show went on, and Fritz got right back to dancing.

• Snow is always pretty complicated, and there are often crazy incidents. Whenever props are in the mix, the chances for problems increase, so there are many snow-scene escapades. I once got my snow puffs tangled up in another girl's. Another time, someone missed their entrance, and they ran on and jumped directly over me while I was posed like this on stage.

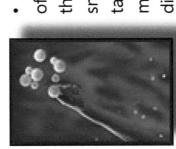

Outside photos: Wade Heninger/Heninger Fotographik. Thank you, Emerald Ballet Theatre.

• It's never happened to me, but I've seen a few snow dumps, where the snow that's supposed to fall gently over the ten-minute dance, somehow all falls in one huge pile, usually on top of a very surprised snowflake.

Things happen. It's best to take it in stride and keep going if you can, and get offstage if you can't. I've seen shoes and straps come undone, crowns fall off, the big shoe throw totally miss the Mouse King, and dancers miss their cues. I even saw a girl break her arm during a performance once. Her partner quickly swooped her up and carried her offstage, and the audience was left wondering whether it was part of the choreography because of his quick thinking.

I'm generally pretty calm, so when a last-minute substitution dancer is needed, I sometimes get a brand-new part. I went in as a surprise party girl one year. I loved hearing my mom describe being in the audience and thinking, "Wow, that girl looks a lot like Konora. Really, just like her. They could be twins. Wait, the girl moves just like her, too. You know, I think that IS Konora!"

All photos this spread: Wade Heninger/Heninger Fotographik. Thank you, Emerald Ballet Theatre.

One year, my friend hurt her leg during the bows one night. She had a really big part, and there wasn't an understudy. Another dancer and I split the choreography. We learned the dances the next morning for that afternoon's show. I had a tutu at home that almost fit, and I wore it for the show. Luckily, there was a lot of solo dancing, so no one knew how many times I messed up.

At Ballet Idaho, there were some last-minute casting shuffles, and I had to dance a part that was similar to a part I knew, but with different counts and places on stage. I think I did pretty well, considering. It wasn't perfect, and I made a couple of mistakes, but if you keep smiling, the audience probably doesn't even notice.

"Just keep dancing" sounds like a good motto for life as well as the stage. I hope I always have dance in my life. It's brought me so much joy, sweat, tears, laughter, friendship, and pride over the years.

Thanks for letting me reflect on my *Nutcrackers*. It was nice to tell you all about it. I hope you get to see *The Nutcracker* on stage sometime. Even if it's sort of a weird story, it's really fun to see all the different costumes and characters.

Love,

♥

Sonora

Until our next adventure,

Keep practicing.

Keep learning.

Fancy French*

- pirouette ['peer-oh-wet'] twirl (whirl/spin)
- sous sus ['su-su'] over-under (or under the above) (might also see *sous sous* or *sus sous*)

  sous sus most often refers to the movement getting into the position
- passé ['pah-SAY'] passed

  passé is the movement, *retiré* is the position, both words are used
- retiré ['reh-tee-RAY'] withdrawn
- arabesque ['air-a-BESK'] a decorative pattern of intertwined flowing lines
- sauté ['so-TAY'] jumped (jumps/jumping)
- tendu ['tawn-DOO'] stretched (might also hear *battement tendu*)
- devant ['duh-VAHn'] in front
- derrière ['deh-REE-air'] behind
- saut de chat ['so-deh-SHAW'] jump of the cat

Other Poses Mentioned

- first position
- splits
- V arms

Coming Up Next

We're working on a couple of books. Grown-ups can subscribe at *www.OnceUponADance.com*. (Watch for subscriber bonus content.)

*Not official pronunciations.

Photos this spread: Wade Heninger/Heninger Fotographik. Thank you, Emerald Ballet Theatre.

Want to make us smile?

We'd love a kind, honest review from a grown-up on Amazon or Goodreads.

Once Upon a Dance is a mother-daughter pandemic collaboration. It would mean so much to know you liked our book.

Most photos this spread: Wade Heninger/Heninger Fotographik. Thank you, Emerald Ballet Theatre.

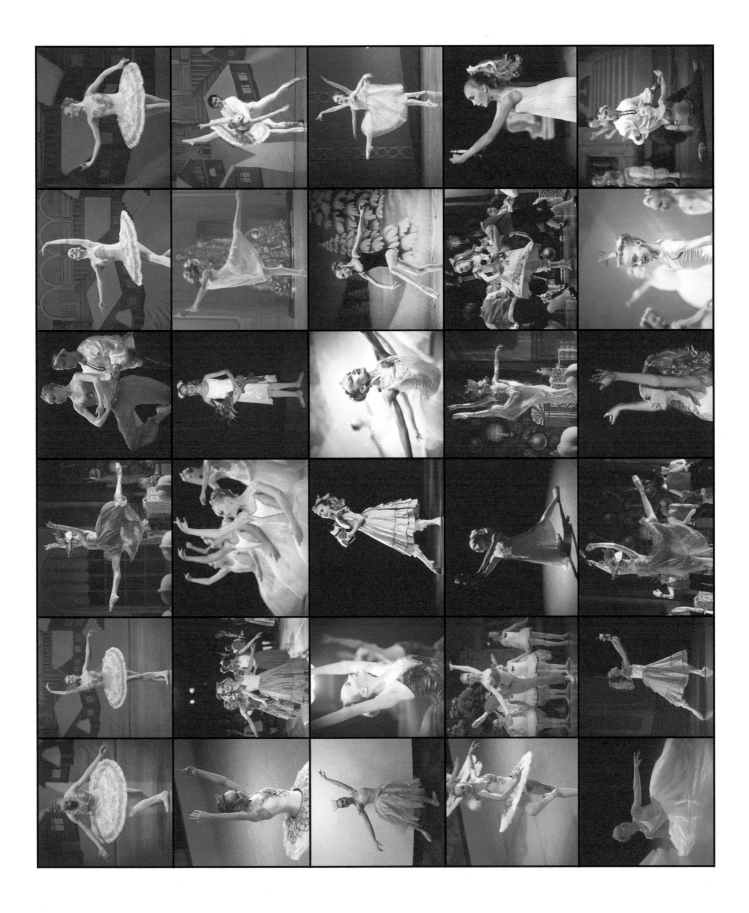

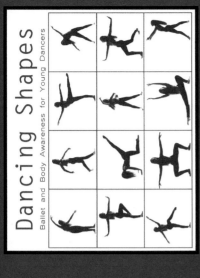

Dancing Shapes
Ballet and Body Awareness for Young Dancers

More Dancing Shapes
Ballet and Body Awareness for Young Dancers

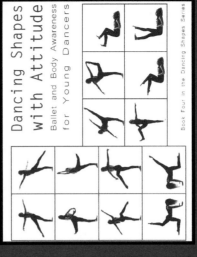

Dancing Shapes with Attitude
Ballet and Body Awareness for Young Dancers

Book Four in the Dancing Shapes Series

Konora's Shapes
Poses from *Dancing Shapes* for Creative Movement & Ballet Teachers

More Konora's Shapes
Poses from *More Dancing Shapes* for Creative Movement & Ballet Teachers

"Beautiful images and creative dance activities! I am so impressed with the quality and concept of this book series (this is our third). The images are crisp and beautiful and the ideas for using the book are SO MUCH FUN!

My kids (age 6-11) and I are having a great time trying out the activity ideas that go with the images. ...The activities are stretching us in many ways: dissecting and recreating poses down to the smallest details, using dance/movement vocabulary, team work, problem solving, thinking creatively, etc..."

www.OnceUponADance.com

Breath
Movement
Imagination!

Dance-It-Out
Creative Movement
Stories for Young Movers

Joel Finds His JUMP!

Petunia Perks Up

2021 Coming Soon:

Princess Naomi Helps a Unicorn

Brielle's Birthday Ball

Danny, Denny, & the Dancing Dragon

The Cat with the Crooked Tail

Danika's Dancing Day